IRVIN L. YOUNG MEMORIAL LIBRARY
W9-AAH-884

LIGHTNING BOLT BOOKS™

The Energy That Warms Us

A Look at Heat

Jennifer Boothroyd

Lerner Publications Company
Minneapolis

To Erin—
a great friend
with a warm
heart!

Lerner Publications Company
A division of Lerner Publishing Group, Inc.
241 First Avenue North
Minneapolis, MN 55401 U.S.A.

Website address: www.lernerbooks.com

Library of Congress Cataloging-in-Publication Data

Boothroyd, Jennifer, 1972-
The energy that warms us: a look at heat / by Jennifer Boothroyd.
p. cm. — (Lightning bolt books ™— Exploring physical science)
Includes index.
ISBN 978-0-7613-6093-3 (lib. bdg. : alk. paper)
1. Heat—Juvenile literature. I. Title.
QC256.B66 2011
536—dc22 2010017066

Manufactured in the United States of America
1 — CG — 12/15/10

Contents

What Is Heat?

Have you felt the warmth of a sunny summer day? Or a mug of hot chocolate? That warmth is heat. **Heat is a form of energy.**

We use heat all the time. Heat is used to cook food. Heat makes a shower or bath warm.

Heat was used to bake this bread.

Heat is also used to make and shape things.

Molten gold is poured into a mold to create a gold bar.

How Heat Is Made

The sun provides heat for all living things. Its energy heats Earth.

Heat also comes from inside Earth. Hot, melted rocks are deep under the ground. Their heat warms rocks and water on the planet.

Steam rises from this hot spring at Yellowstone National Park. Hot springs are pools of water heated by Earth.

Friction is a force created when two things rub together. Friction makes heat.

Heather rubs her hands together to stay warm.

Fire makes heat. People use heat from fire to cook their food. Sometimes they make fires to stay warm outside in cold weather.

A family uses the heat from a campfire to roast marshmallows.

Our bodies turn the food we eat into energy. Some of that energy is turned into heat.

Derek uses his energy to play soccer. He gets very warm when he plays.

How Heat Moves

Heat moves in three ways. Heat travels in liquids and gases by convection.

Convection often makes the air cooler and windier near the ocean.

Convection carries heat through a pot of water on the stove.

Water keeps moving around in a pot as shown above until all the water is equally warm.

Convection also moves heat through gases in the air.

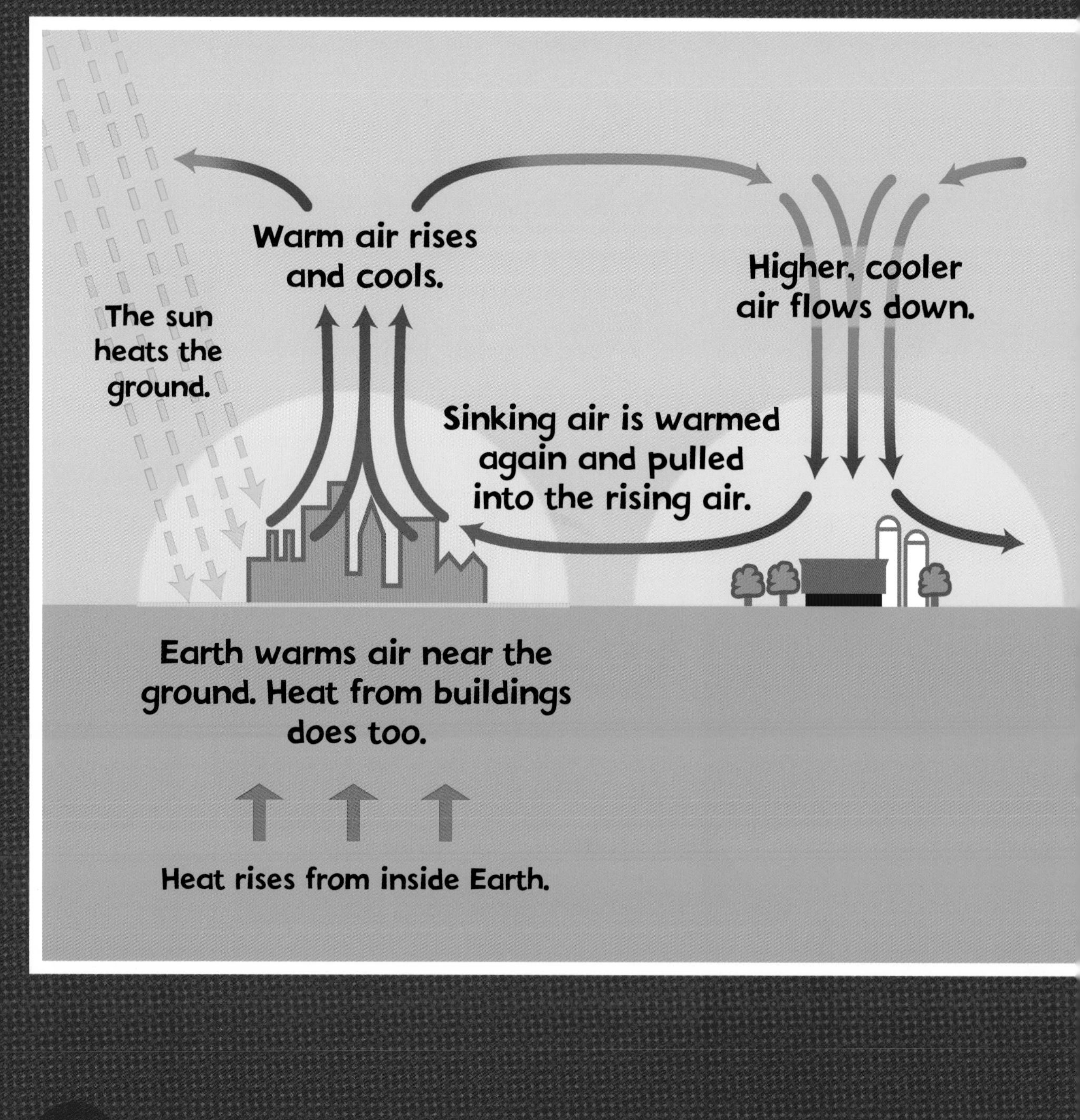

Conduction carries heat between objects that are touching.

This spoon will become hot after sitting in a bowl of hot soup for a few minutes.

Metal is a good conductor of heat. Heat travels through metal quickly. Wood is not a very good conductor. Heat takes longer to travel through wood.

This wooden board keeps the metal pan's heat from burning the tablecloth.

Heat travels through space by radiation. The heat moves in rays we cannot see.

Planets closer to the sun get more of its heat than faraway planets do.

How Heat Is Measured

The amount of heat in an object is its temperature. Cold objects have low temperatures. Hot objects have high temperatures.

Snow cones have low temperatures. They can cool you off on a hot day!

A thermometer is a tool that measures temperature.

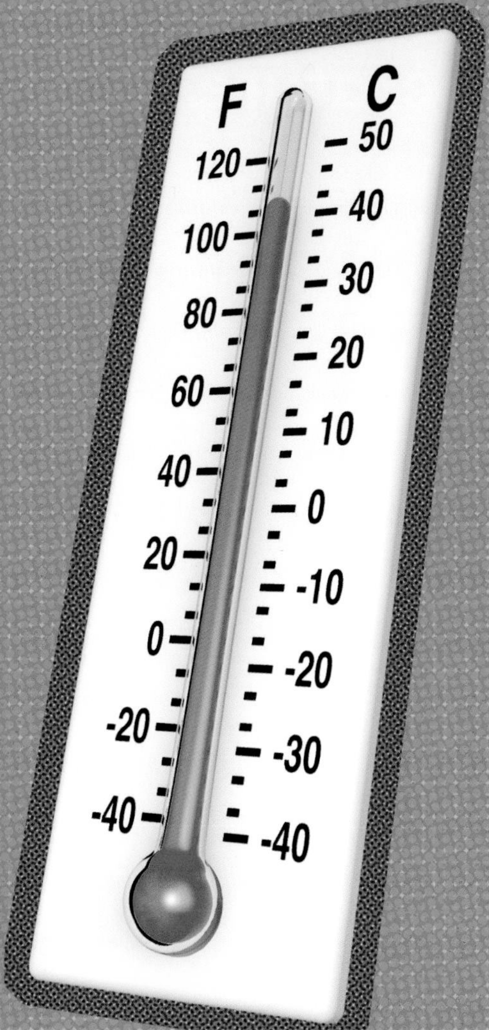

Temperature is usually measured in degrees Fahrenheit or degrees Celsius.

We use thermometers to measure the air outside. We use thermometers to measure the temperature of food too.

We know that meat is cooked when it reaches a certain temperature.

We also use a thermometer to measure our body temperature.

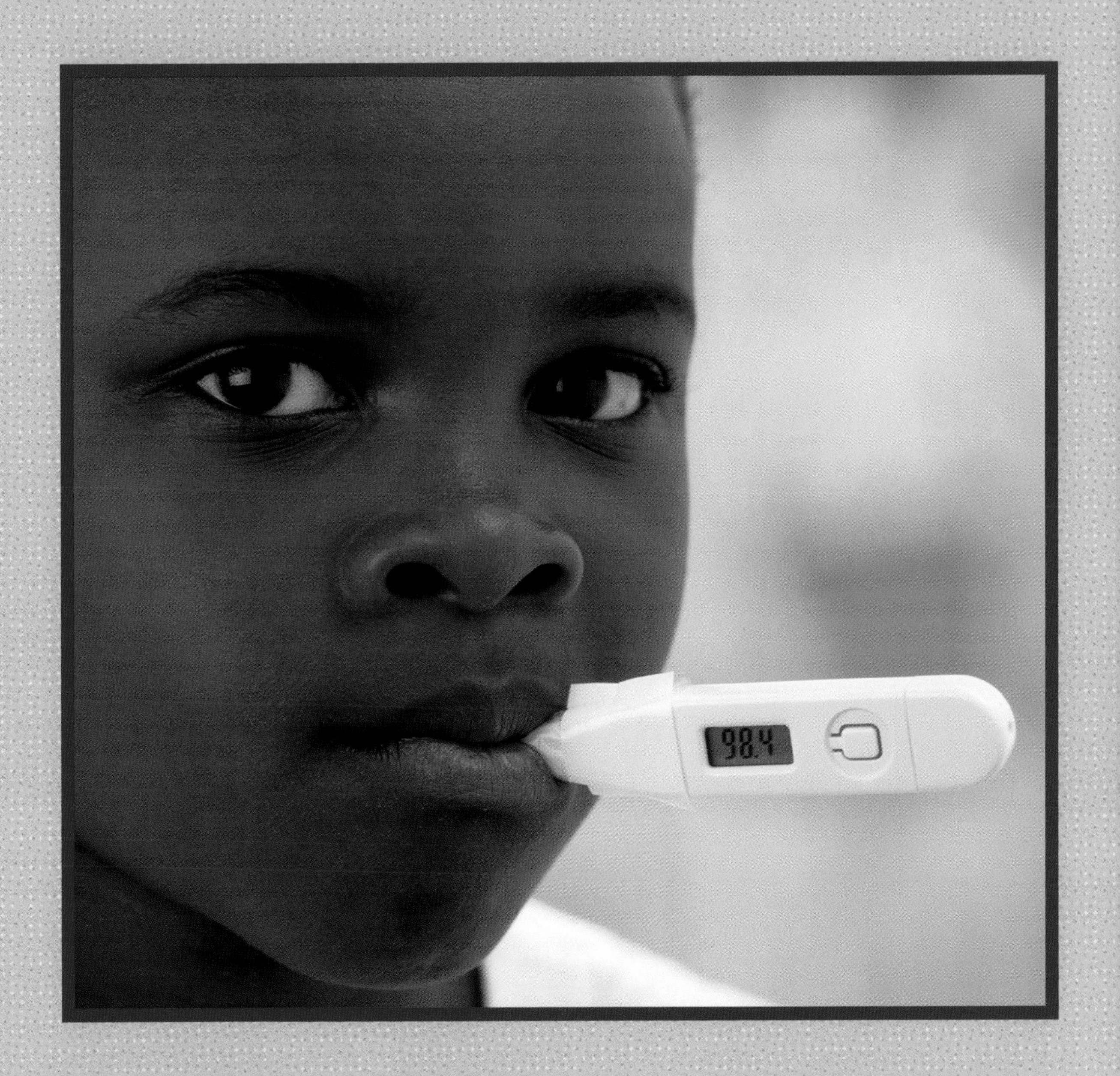

Balancing Hot and Cold

Living things need to stay warm. Clothing and blankets keep the heat of our bodies from escaping into the air. People wear thick clothing when it is cold. Birds depend on their feathers to keep warm. Mammals have hair or fur.

It can be dangerous if living things get too hot. But people and animals have ways to keep their bodies the right temperature. Some animals have much thinner coats of fur during warmer months.

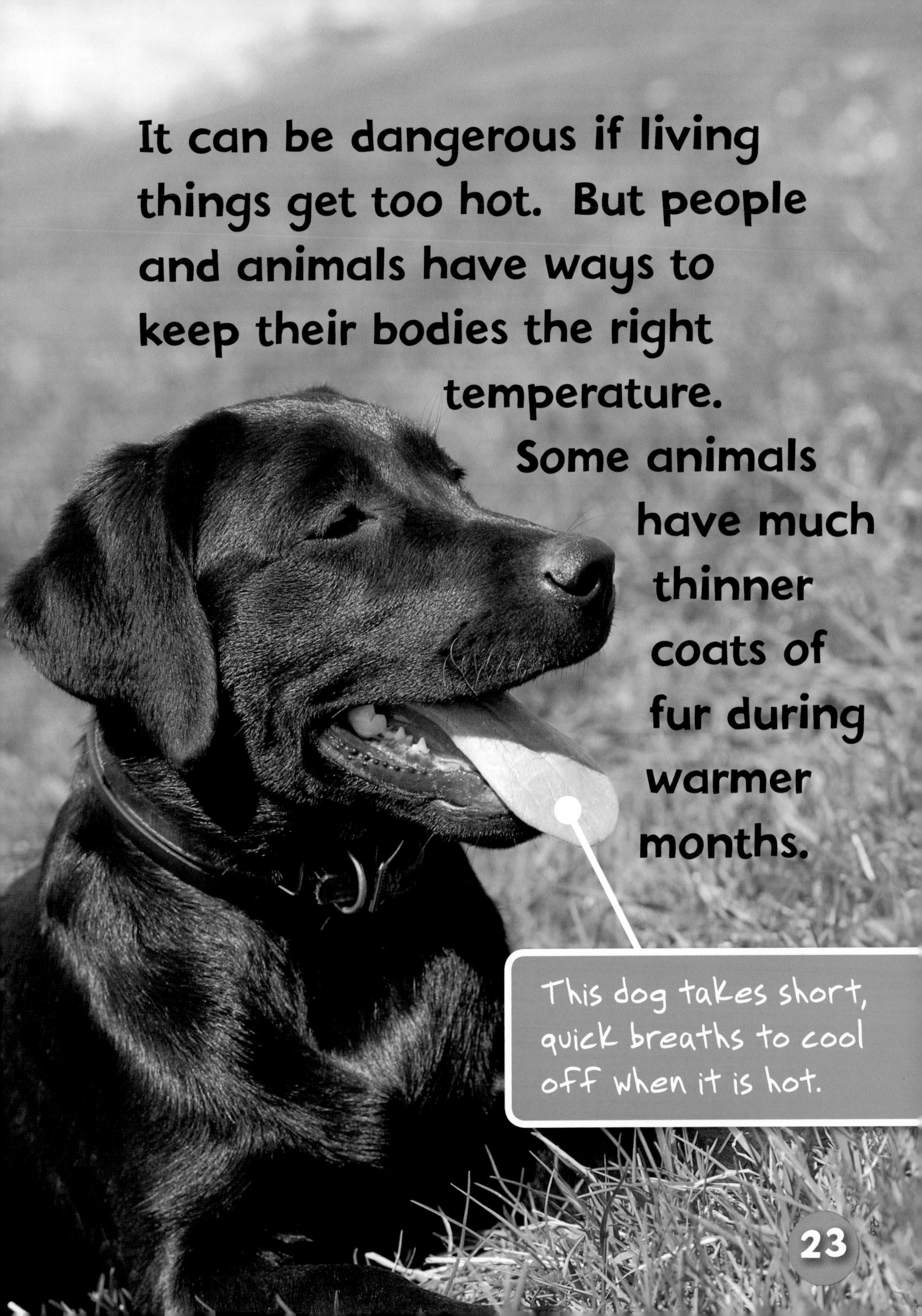

This dog takes short, quick breaths to cool off when it is hot.

People wear thin, loose clothing in hot weather. Then air can move the heat away from our bodies.

Light-colored clothing stays cooler in sunlight than dark clothing does.

People also have ways to control the temperature indoors. **An air conditioner takes heat out of the air.** That makes the air cooler.

A furnace heats the air. And insulation acts like a blanket for walls and roofs. It keeps hot or cold air in and the outside air out.

This man puts insulation in the walls and ceiling of a home.

How do you stay warm or cool enough?

Activity
Big Air

Heat causes gases to expand, or spread out. Try this experiment to trap expanding air!

What you need:

latex balloon

plastic bottle

2 large bowls

sink

What you do:

1. Stretch the balloon over the top of the bottle.
2. Fill one of the bowls halfway with cold water from the sink.
3. Fill the other bowl halfway with hot water from the sink.
4. Put the bottom of the bottle into the bowl of hot water, and hold it in place. Be careful not to touch the hot water! Watch what happens to the balloon.
5. Put the bottom of the bottle into the bowl of cold water, and hold it in place. Watch what happens to the balloon.

Did the balloon seem to fill up with more air when the bottle was in the hot water? The heat of the water should have caused the air in the bottle to warm. As it warmed, it would expand into the balloon. Then the cold water should have caused the air to cool again.

Glossary

conduction: a process by which heat moves through a solid, a liquid, or a gas

convection: a way of moving heat through a liquid or a gas. The warmer parts rise, and the colder parts sink.

degree: a unit for measuring temperature

friction: a force that makes heat. Rubbing creates friction.

furnace: a machine that creates heat. Furnaces are used to heat buildings.

insulation: a material that stops heat from moving through it

radiation: energy in the form of waves or particles. Light, heat, and X-rays all travel through radiation.

temperature: the amount of heat in an object

thermometer: a tool that measures temperature

Further Reading

BrainPOP Jr.: Heat
http://www.brainpopjr.com/science/energy/heat/grownups.weml

Convection, Conduction, and Radiation
http://www.mansfieldct.org/schools/mms/staff/hand/convcondrad.htm

Mahaney, Ian F. *Heat.* New York: Rosen, 2007.

Rivera, Sheila. *Heating.* Minneapolis: Lerner Publications Company, 2007.

The Space Place: Beat the Heat!
http://spaceplace.nasa.gov/en/kids/st8/thermal_loop

Walker, Sally M. *Heat.* Minneapolis: Lerner Publications Company, 2006.

Index

Photo Acknowledgments

The images in this book are used with the permission of: © iStockphoto.com/Dean Turner, p. 1; © SuperStock RF/SuperStock, p. 2; © iStockphoto.com/Pathathai Chungyam, p. 4; © iStockphoto.com/Kelly Cline, p. 5; © Chuck Nacke/Alamy, p. 6; © iStockphoto.com/frankoppermann, p. 7; © TMI/Alamy, p. 8; © iStockphoto.com/Daniela Jovanovska-Hristovska, p. 9; © Ariel Skelly/Blend Images/Getty Images, p. 10; © Photo and Co/Getty Images, p. 11; © iStockphoto.com/Jaren Wicklund, p. 12; © Laura Westlund/Independent Picture Service, pp. 13, 14; © iStockphoto.com/Ingrid Heczko, p. 15; © iStockphoto.com/Stephanie Howard, p. 16; © Stocktrek Images/Getty Images, p. 17; © Enigma/Alamy, p. 18; © iStockphoto.com/Terry Morris, p. 19; © Cusp/SuperStock, p. 20; © Authur Tilley/Woodbook Stock/Getty Images, p. 21; © Andy Rouse/Minden Pictures, p. 22; © Himrina/Dreamstime.com, p. 23; © iStockphoto.com/Eileen Hart, p. 24; © Marka/Alamy, p. 25; © PM Images/Iconica/Getty Images, p. 26; © LWA/The Image Bank/Getty Images, p. 27; © iStockphoto.com/t3000, p. 28, (plastic water bottle); © Freddy Eliasson/Shutterstock Images, p. 28, (empty purple balloon); © Alex Staroseltsev/Shutterstock Images,pg 28, (fish bowl); © David R. Frazier/Alamy, p. 30, 31 (top); © Ian Shaw/Alamy, p. 31 (bottom).

Front cover: © Roger Harris/SPL/Getty Images.